# PIANO PIECES THE WHOLE WORLD PLAYS

Containing more than seventy compositions
dear to the hearts of piano lovers, representing
the finest creations of such noted composers as

| | | |
|---|---|---|
| BACH | GRIEG | RACHMANINOFF |
| BEETHOVEN | LANGE | RUBINSTEIN |
| BOHM | MACDOWELL | SAINT-SAËNS |
| BRAHMS | MASCAGNI | SCHARWENKA |
| CHAMINADE | MASSENET | SCHUBERT |
| CHOPIN | MOSZKOWSKI | SCHUMANN |
| DVOŘÁK | MENDELSSOHN | TSCHAIKOWSKY |
| GODARD | MOZART | VERDI |
| GOUNOD | PADEREWSKI | WAGNER |

Presented in the original, unabridged editions

Selected and Edited
by

## ALBERT E. WIER

Amsco Publications
New York/London/Sydney

L. M. FURTADO & CO.
BOMBAY - 400 002.

International Standard Book Number: 0.8256.1000.1

*Exclusive Distributors:*
Music Sales Corporation
225 Park Avenue South, New York, NY 10003 USA
Music Sales Limited
8/9 Frith Street, London W1V 5TZ England
Music Sales Pty. Limited
120 Rothschild Street, Rosebery, Sydney NSW 2018 Australia

Printed in the United States of America by
Vicks Lithograph and Printing Corporation

# To the Piano Lover

LOVERS of piano music have many moods—hence this collection of piano compositions designed to please the most variant tastes. From classical masters to modern geniuses—from Bach and Tschaikowsky to lighter masters such as Poldini—each page will unfold new beauties to those who seek the piano in their recreative hours. Those who possess it will not be long in realizing that this volume is a treasure-trove of truly inexhaustible wealth.

THE EDITOR

# Classified Index

## CLASSIC PIANO PIECES

## MODERN PIANO PIECES

## LIGHT PIANO PIECES

## OPERATIC PIANO PIECES

# Alphabetical Index

# Composers' Index

# Nocturne
## E-FLAT MAJOR

F. CHOPIN Op. 9 № 2

8

# Serenade

## (Ständchen)

FR. SCHUBERT

# Cradle Song

M. HAUSER

# Gipsy Rondo

J. HAYDN

18

Minore

# Spring Song
### "Song without Words," No. XXX

Allegretto grazioso

F. MENDELSSOHN
Op.62, No.6

# Prelude in C
## Welltempered Clavichord

J. S. BACH

Allegro

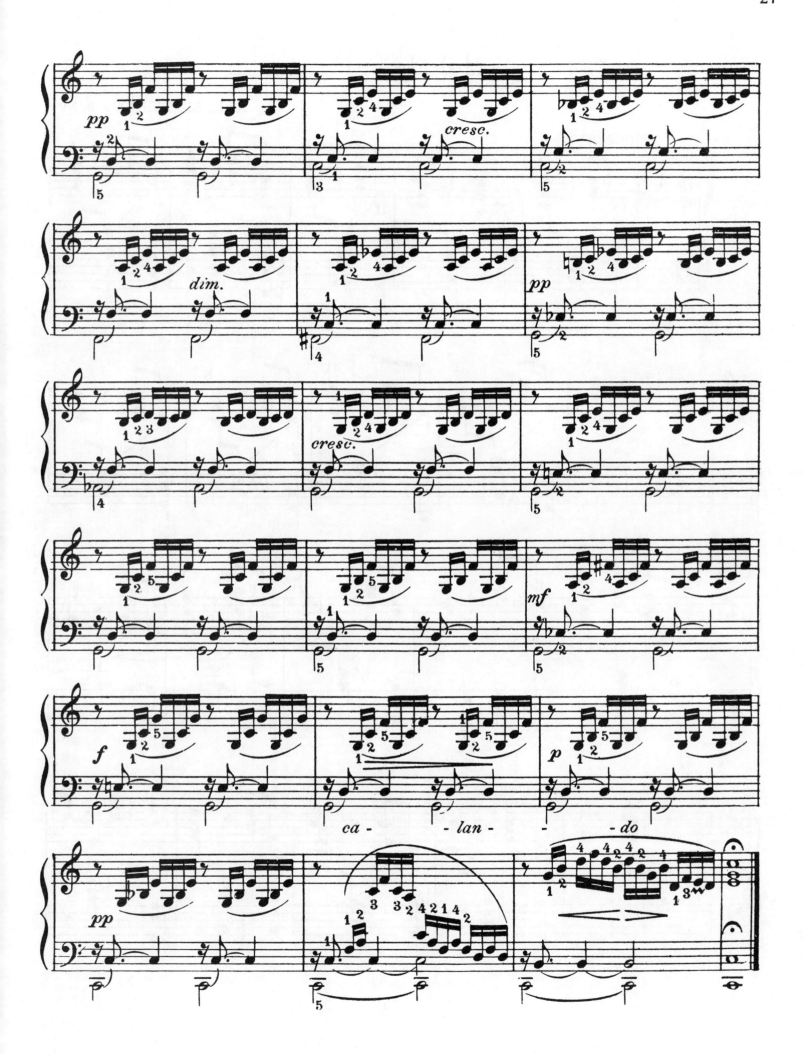

# Melody in F

A. RUBINSTEIN Op. 3, № 1

Moderato

30

# Waltz
## D-FLAT, "THE MINUTE"

F. CHOPIN Op. 64, No. 1

34

# Moment Musical

Fr. SCHUBERT. Op. 94, № 3

# Turkish March

W. A. MOZART

39

# Gavotte

F. J. GOSSEC

Allegretto

# Träumerei.

R. SCHUMANN. Op. 15, No 7.

Moderato

# Little Romance

R. SCHUMANN Op. 68, No. 19

Piú moto

D.C. Traumerei

# Confidence

FELIX MENDELSSOHN, Op. 19, No. 4

# Prélude
## B MINOR

F. CHOPIN. Op. 28, Nº 6

## Prélude
### A MAJOR

F. CHOPIN. Op. 28, № 7

# Für Elise

L. von BEETHOVEN

# Fifth Nocturne

J. LEYBACH

Allegretto

59

# Poupée Valsante

## (DANCING DOLL)

ED. POLDINI

Tempo di Valse

63

# The Flatterer
## La Lisonjera

CECILE CHAMINADE

Moderato molto capriccioso

mf marcato · rubato · rapido · pp · R.H. · L.H · mp · cresc. · f · dolce · p · molto stringendo · dim. e rit. pp

# Humoreske

ANTON DVOŘÁK Op. 101, N? 7

Poco lento e grazioso

Più lento

# Anitra's Dance

EDVARD GRIEG

**Tempo di Mazurka**

74

# Chant sans Paroles

Allegretto grazioso e cantabile

P. TSCHAIKOWSKY
Op. 2, No. 3

# Hungarian Dance
## F-SHARP MINOR, No.5

JOHANNES BRAHMS

# To the Moon

## (FOREST IDYL № 3)

E. A. MACDOWELL

Andante

# Le Cygne

C. SAINT-SAËNS

# Menuet à l' Antique

IGNACE J. PADEREWSKI
Op. 14 , No. 1

88

# Polish Dance

### E-FLAT MINOR

XAVER SCHARWENKA
Op. 3, No. 1

Allegro

# Scarf Dance

# Serenata

M. MOSZKOWSKI
Op. 15, No. 1

Andante grazioso

# Prélude
## C-SHARP MINOR

S. RACHMANINOFF. Op. 3, № 2

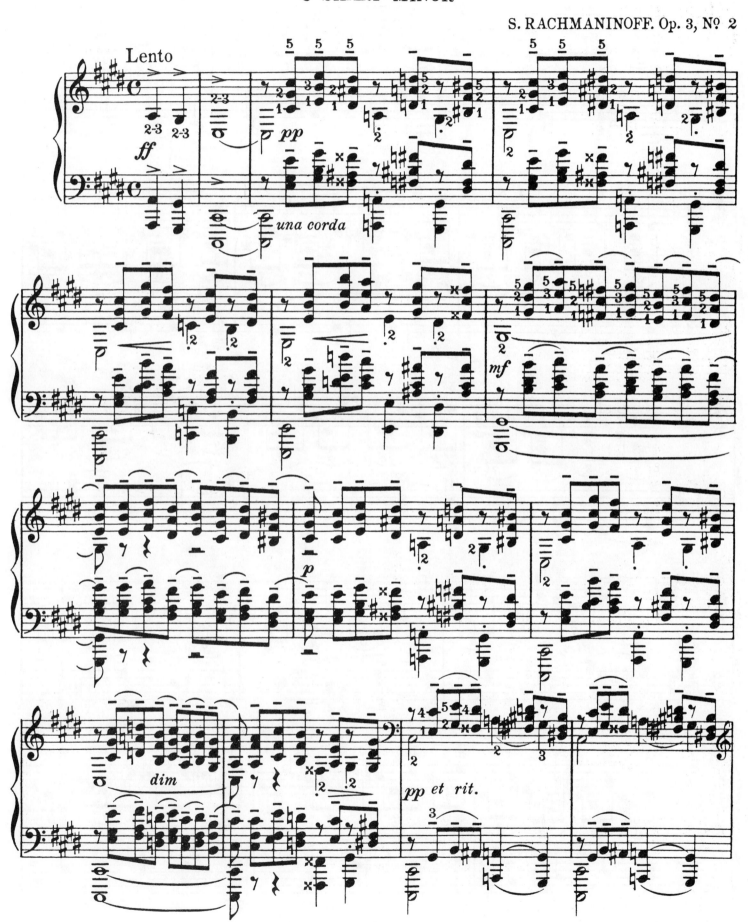

Tempo I.

# Salut d'Amour

EDWARD ELGAR

108

# Valse Bleue

ALFRED MARGIS

INTRODUCTION
Tempo di Valse

# Simple Aveu

FRANCIS THOMÉ

# Flower Song

GUSTAV LANGE

Lento moderato
*cantabile*

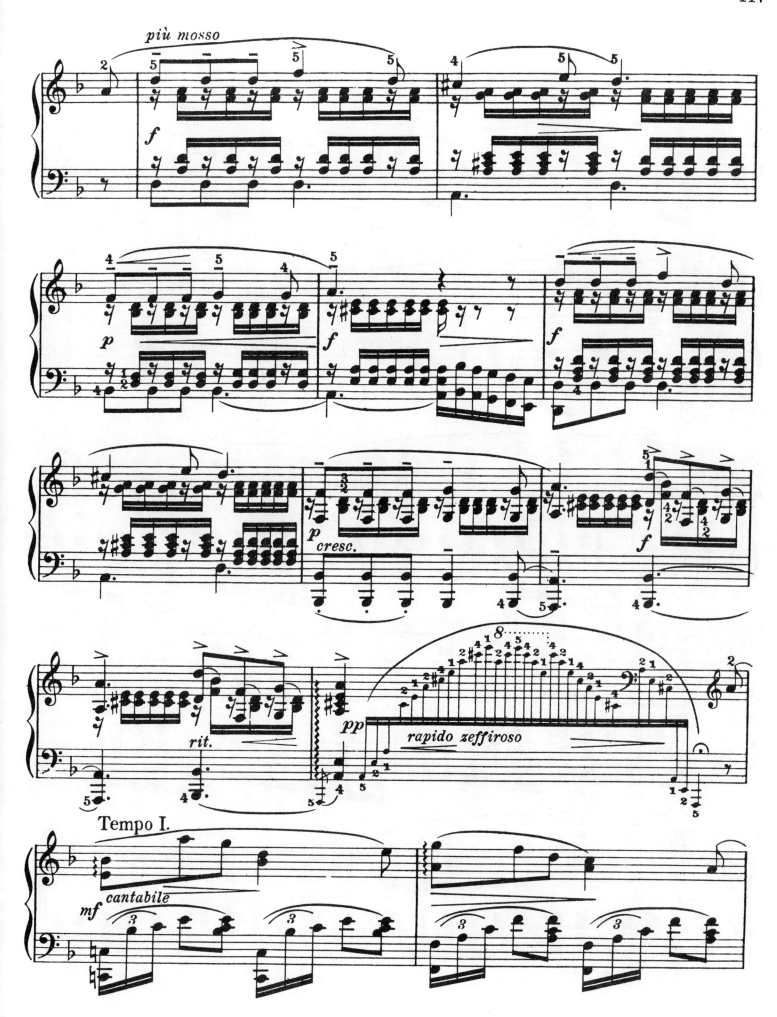

**Tempo I.**

# La Fontaine

## MORCEAU de SALON

C. BOHM

Allegretto

# Longing for Home

## (HEIMWEH)

ALBERT JUNGMANN

Andante con espressione.

# Love's Dream After the Ball

## INTERMEZZO

Returned from the ball, she falls asleep,
and in a charming vision, beholds him to
whom she has given her heart this night.

ALPHONSE CZIBULKA

132

134

# La Cinquantaine

## THE GOLDEN WEDDING

GABRIEL-MARIE

# La Czarine

## RUSSIAN MAZURKA

LOUIS GANNE

140

# Valsette

Allegro

FELIX BOROWSKI

# Le Secret

## INTERMEZZO PIZZICATO

L. GAUTIER

146

D.S. 𝄋 al ⊕ to Coda

# La Paloma

S. YRADIER

Andante con moto.

# Stephanie

## Gavotte

ALPHONSE CZIBULKA

# Thine Own

GUSTAV LANGE

# Love Song

A. HENSELT

Allegretto sostenuto ed amoroso
*molto cantabile*

# Valse Serenade

E. POLDINI

# An Alexis

Arr. by J. N. HUMMEL

Andantino espressivo

# Charge Of The Hussars

FRITZ SPINDLER

**Allegro brillante**

# Gavotte
### (Mignon)

Tempo di Gavotte

A. THOMAS

# Consolation

FRANZ LISZT

# Quartet
## (Rigoletto)

G. VERDI

# Grand March
### (Norma)

V. BELLINI

Tempo di Marcia

# Barcarolle
## (The Tales of Hoffman)

J. OFFENBACH

Moderato

# Aragonaise
## (Le Cid)

JULES MASSENET

# Berceuse
## (Jocelyn)

BENJAMIN GODARD

Andantino

# Dance Of The Hours
## (La Gioconda)

A. PONCHIELLI

# My Heart At Thy Sweet Voice

(Samson and Delilah)

C. SAINT SAËNS

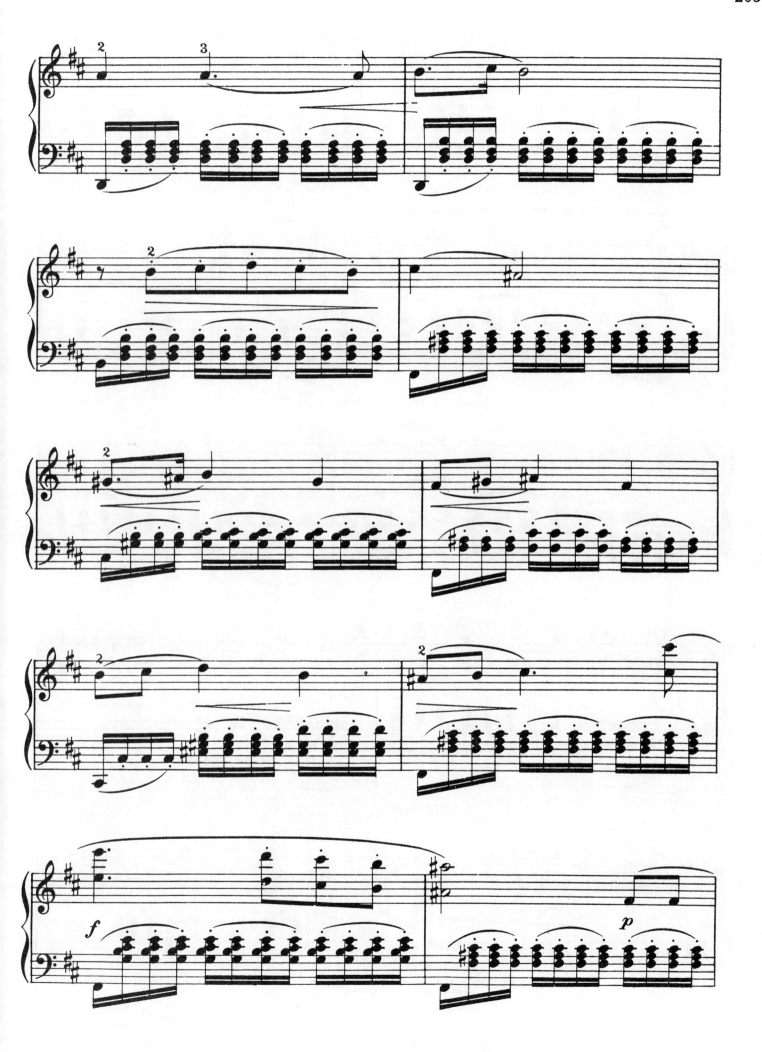

# To The Evening Star
## (Tannhäuser)

R. WAGNER

Andante sostenuto

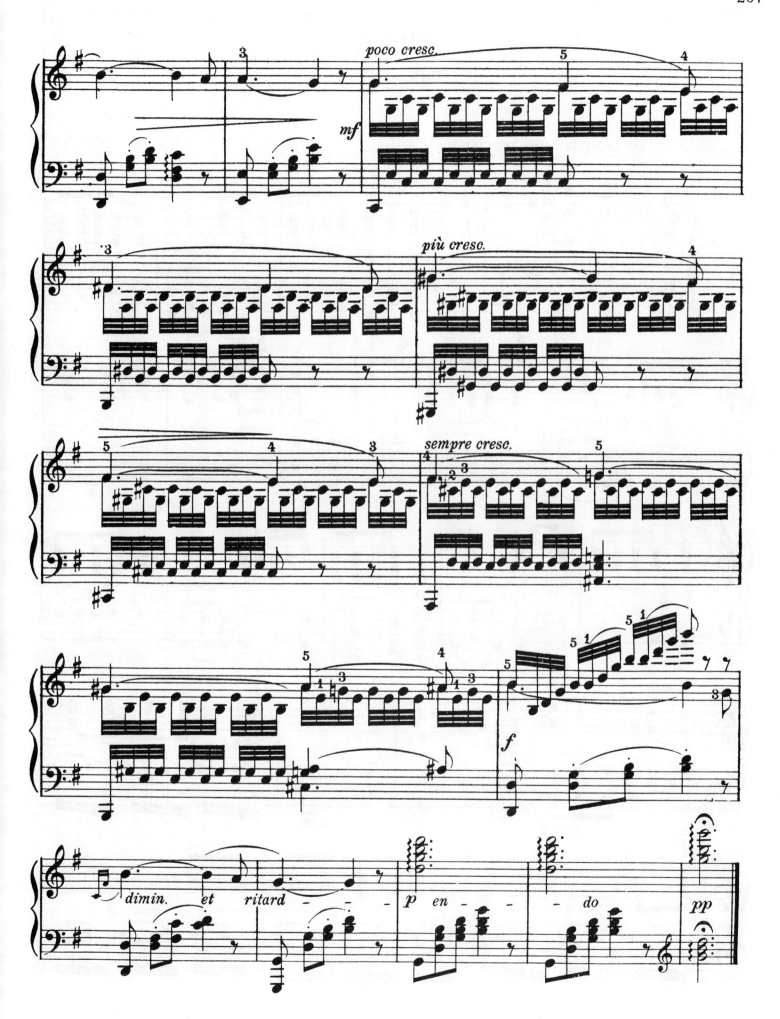

# Minuet

## (DON JUAN)

Andante ma non troppo

W. A. MOZART

# Pizzicato
## ("Sylvia" Ballet)

LÉO DELIBES

# Sextette
## (LUCIA DI LAMMERMOOR)

G. DONIZETTI

# Waltz
## (FAUST)

CH. GOUNOD

Tempo di Valse

# Miserere
## (Il Trovatore)

G. VERDI

Andante